Girls in Science:
Voices for Change

Tips for Equality and Inclusion in Schools,
Workplaces, and Communities

KIM COOPER

Cover by Jill Monsod

Proceeds of this book will be donated to *FIRST* Robotics Canada's
Equity, Diversity, and Inclusivity (EDI) programs.

ISBN: 9781723807978

DEDICATION

To the Girls in STEM Student Council, who share, inspire, and act. And to Dr. Imogen Coe who speaks louder than anyone so that even the silent voices can be heard.

Praise for *Girls in Science: Voices for Change*

"This book is required reading for anyone who wants to see our next generation of young scientists succeed—from parents to educators to community leaders, *Girls in Science: Voices for Change* contains practical information on how we can all contribute to changing the culture of STEM for our children. By sharing girls' stories in their own voices, Kim Cooper gives us an eye-opening look at the challenges our young women face in engaging with STEM activities and the role we as a society play in perpetuating those challenge. Nevertheless, Kim's voice and the girls' voices also reveal tremendous potential for change. With helpful suggestions for change and tips for action that anyone can begin incorporating into their life, *Girls in Science: Voices for Change* sets out a powerful agenda for transformation, and gives us a blueprint for a better, more inclusive future."
—Dr. Jennifer Gardy, Senior Scientist, Associate Professor, Science-television Host, and Children's Book Author

"Girls in Science: Voices for Change takes a candid look at the realities of women in STEM. Through the voices of girls in youth-serving science and technology programs like *FIRST*, we can further understand some of the challenges they face today and how we can work together to create the kind of culture where everyone, no matter their circumstances, can thrive. This book is an excellent resource for schools, teams, and corporations to start and continue conversations about establishing and maintaining accepting environments. Kim Cooper provides practical tips and inspirational next steps towards creating caring, inclusive communities that inspire innovation."
—Don Bossi, President of *FIRST*

"Girls face different challenges around the world. It's critical that we as a society try to better understand the different barriers for women on a global scale so we can make change. *Girls in Science: Voices for Change* will spark honest conversations about obstacles, collaborations and allies. If we don't listen to the many voices trying to be heard, we will never truly progress and work towards making this world a better place."
—Dr. Roya Mahboob, Innovator, Entrepreneur, and CEO of Digital Citizen Fund

Contents

Introduction

If we want to make change, we require the courage to use our voices. And we also need the courage to listen. Listening to others who come from different backgrounds or who are systematically left out of the conversation can help us transcend limitations. If we fail to listen to girls in science and act now, we will be missing out on talent, opportunities, and innovation.

There's a serious lack of equality, diversity, and inclusion in the science, technology, engineering, and math (STEM) fields. By maintaining the status quo, we are guilty of ignoring that race, gender, ethnicity, and socioeconomic factors remain barriers to entry and continuation in the STEM fields. The systemic issues involved are multifaceted and often overwhelming. But we, as a society, have an incredible opportunity to take steps to promote inclusivity that will lead to more collaboration, brilliance, and groundbreaking advancements which will not only make this world a better place but also further our understanding of one another, improve goodwill towards others, and make society richer on many levels.

Girls in science can help. By sharing their stories and communicating the current barriers to girls, boys, teachers, parents, mentors, executives, and all stakeholders, we can take steps for change. *Girls in Science: Voices for Change* will not only inspire fresh ideas on equity and diversity based on youthful thinking, it will also present tangible and practical guidelines for inclusion.

The Voices of Inspiration

I work as the lead partnership liaison at *FIRST* Robotics Canada—a charity encouraging kids and youth in STEM. (*FIRST* stands for "For Inspiration and Recognition of Science and Technology.") What sparked my interest and passion in STEM were the talented young people who are involved in this program. These students are the kind of extraordinary people who we want to lead our country, change policies, and create a vibrant culture of inclusivity. Those in underrepresented communities face real struggles, must deal with challenging stereotypes, and face adversities in fields such as STEM. It was these inspirational people who made me join the massive initiative to champion equality and inclusivity.

Research shows that girls are interested in STEM but they, and other underrepresented groups, are getting pushed out of the field. We're not creating a welcoming environment accepting of diversity, nor are we building a strong collaborative network of girls and boys who have the skills and mindset to work together. But why does it matter? If we create the kind of environment where girls and boys collaborate and contribute, these future leaders will be able to see issues from multiple viewpoints and work collectively, ultimately resulting in more profitability and opportunities. We need girls and boys from a vast array of backgrounds to help change this world and make it a better place.

When I first dreamed of an inspirational retreat for high school girls in the *FIRST* Robotics Competition program, I approached Mark Breadner, the president of the organization, about it. Half expecting to hear the improbabilities and obstacles to executing such an event, I was absolutely blown away by his committed and enthusiastic affirmation to move forward: "Love the idea. Let's do it." In just one moment, suddenly my little concept became a colossal and compelling project—that was also wildly intimidating. Mark recommended I ask for John Abele's advice. John is the cofounder of medical device company Boston Scientific and founder of the Argosy Foundation, an organization that supports people and programs which make our society a better place. John is an influencer of change and asks all the right questions when it comes to the toughest problems.

During my first phone conversation with John, one of the most memorable things he said was, "When we're talking about inclusion for girls in STEM, we have to start with changing culture. That's a tough thing to do." His words resonated with me and the more we talked, the more I realized that he was absolutely right. Sure, we can attract more girls into STEM fields but changing the culture in order to welcome, accept, and embrace these girls so they can thrive and make a difference is most definitely going to be a challenge. However, it is one that I, and everyone at *FIRST* Robotics Canada, am not going to shy away from.

It was shortly before my conversation with John that I had met Dr. Imogen Coe, renowned scientist and former dean of science at Ryerson University. She instantly became my role model. She has character and presence, and she commands attention in any room. She is also a staunch promoter of equity, diversity, and inclusivity in STEM. In fact, she works tirelessly to try and change STEM culture to create a more welcoming environment for all. I invited her to be the keynote speaker at the Girls in FIRST Weekend retreat, joining other strong role models such as FIRST Robotics Canada chair of the board of directors Dorothy Byers, CEO of Holland Bloorview Kids Rehabilitation Hospital Julia Hanigsberg, and General Motors Canada engineering team leader Stephanie Thompson. The event was sponsored by John's Argosy Foundation and General Motors Canada, a corporation full of passionate changemakers who are striving for a level of respect and equality for women that strongly aligns with the principles of FIRST.

Then I crossed paths with my biggest catalyst—girls in STEM. The Girls in FIRST Weekend allowed me to connect on a deeper level to a diverse group of girls and listen to their experiences in the program and in STEM, and to hear about the turmoil they have within themselves. It was during that weekend that I truly came to understand the systemic issues and very real struggles they face, and the multitude of people in these girls' circles who are resisting change and making it impossible for them to want to stay and thrive in STEM. I heard their voices loud and clear. The divides go much deeper than gender—interwoven with it are also issues of race, cultural expectations, and socioeconomic factors. This combination results in incredibly unique individual experiences. The more we can understand the multitude of factors influencing these young women, the more we can try to break down the layers of challenges for both girls and boys. Although I'm starting with girls in STEM, it doesn't stop there. We all need to become more sensitive to the prejudices and obstacles that exist for all.

John Abele talks about the power of harnessing collective intelligence, and it was during this weekend that I realized that right in front of me were the difference-makers with the mind power and talent to help take steps to change the culture around them. But let's be clear, it's not only girls who face barriers in STEM: it's girls and boys from underserved communities including newcomers, visible minorities, LGBTQ2, First Nations, and a host of other people who do not come from a place of privilege. John was absolutely right that changing the culture is going to be difficult, often seemingly impossible. But there's no turning back. These talented young minds are part of a generation that can do anything—they've already proven it. They build robots in six weeks, they travel to Africa to teach kids' engineering concepts with LEGO, they register patents at the age of fourteen, and they have a mindset that all barriers are temporary. They are the ones who CAN change the culture. They are the ones who can prove that boys and girls, and men and women, from diverse backgrounds can collaborate, innovate, and build stronger foundations for the next generations.

So how do we help these young minds make a change? We listen. We listen so intently that their voices echo in our minds every day. We listen to the girls, boys, mentors, sponsors—everyone who is a stakeholder. Then we strategize. We work together with the same group to take progress one step further. And we work with corporations to evaluate what's working and not working for them in their industries. Let's learn from STEM industries, and encourage these industries to learn from our youth.

Sharing Their Stories

There was a group of girls who approached me individually following the Girls in *FIRST* Weekend to express interest in getting more involved. They wanted to take what they had learned (and felt) during the weekend, continue to inspire and brainstorm, and move one step further. I decided to replicate the adult version of the *FIRST* Robotics Canada Girls in STEM Executive Advisory Council for students; our new council comprised the nine girls who had approached me to make a change. The girls, who are all part of *FIRST* Robotics Competition (FRC) teams, have taught me so much about strength and resilience, and they demonstrate the kind of diversity of thought that we need in society. Thank you to Ishra, Alexandra, Jessica, Mehakdeep, Paulina, Eileen, Erica, Madison, and Kouthar, who all come from diverse backgrounds and bravely face different challenges related to race, ethnicity, gender, and other factors. By hearing their voices, I have been inspired to hope that we can make a difference—in fact, we are making a difference. This collective passion and striving for a common goal motivates us to act—which is exactly my intention with this book.

My hope is that this book will inspire steps—no matter how big or small—toward change. I also hope that it will spark fresh conversations and ideas. The content is broken down into digestible sections with tips for students, mentors, teachers, kids, sponsors, and all stakeholders. There are secrets to building stronger teams, tips to working towards a more accepting mindset, and better communication strategies to help create a more inclusive environment. The best part about it? This book is wholly inspired by the voices of youth and backed by the next generation of leaders who know the secret to innovation and making this world a better place.

Are you ready to take the next step in changing our culture? Read on to hear the voices of girls in STEM and find out how you can make changes within your organization, school, club, corporation, community . . . and within yourself.

Chapter 1: Out of the Womb

I t's a boy! It's a girl! We've all said or heard these statements in some capacity when it comes to the joy of welcoming a newborn into this world. But along with those words creep in traditional stereotypes. These include relationships to colours. We have been conditioned to think of blue for boys and pink for girls.

> "When my friends start having babies, I will not give them any pink or blue gifts simply because I want nothing to do with these girl and boy stereotypes. I like the colour pink but not because they say it's for girls. I like it because I like it. Period."
>
> —Anj, Grade 10 student

So what happens if you give a pink-coloured onesie as a shower gift to a proud mama of a baby boy? Blasphemy! Some mamas are horrified. How can her newborn baby boy wear pink? But considering that pink used to be a masculine colour, it's ironic that somehow it is now directly equated with girls. But a colour is a colour—and only that. Look beyond stereotypes and make choices you like, no matter the colour. If you have to explain why you chose that particular shade, then be proud and announce it to everyone.

For example, take this scenario:

Gift receiver: "Why on earth would you buy my baby girl a blue onesie with the words FUTURE DIESEL MECHANIC on the front?"

Gift giver: "Are you kidding me? She may be your only hope to get that rusted VW out of your driveway before the next century."

Gift Receiver: "Good point. Did you get her a hoist and toolbox too?"

There's a good chance you've never experienced or witnessed anything remotely close to that situation, and if you have, there's more chance the gift was a joke and not intended to be meaningful. But what if it wasn't so off-base? What if girls were given more opportunity to build concrete skills, such as the know-how to fix cars? What if society was less concerned about fitting little ones into traditional categories and more into letting boys and girls gravitate towards what they like without limitations? We need to take small steps to begin changing perceptions—and even something like colours can make a difference.

FIRST Robotics Canada staff can choose from two colours of work shirt with the FIRST logo embroidered on the left side: the shirts come in black and pink. The president of the organization always chooses the pink over the black as he wants to support girls in STEM and he can demonstrate that by wearing the pink shirt. Every time I see that pink shirt on Mark (and that's often, because we have a lot of events), I'm proud to work for the organization and have him as my boss—not only because he feels he's supporting girls in STEM by wearing pink, but because he's a man of influence and respect who's breaking the lingering stereotype about how men shouldn't wear pink. At first, spectators made a few comments about his shirt, but as time went on, the pink shirt was normalized. I repeat: the pink shirt was normalized. Now it is completely normal for Mark (and other male staff members) to wear pink. Mark Breadner is changing the culture, one pink shirt at a time.

There's a high school robotics team in Toronto called the Pink Titans that is composed of both boys and girls. They have bright pink team shirts, marketing material, and sometimes even wigs. They chose the colour pink to signify key characteristics of their team, including acceptance, hopefulness, optimism, playfulness, and youthfulness. Their trademark pink has also become completely normalized within the FIRST community. This group is showing that pink isn't just for girls—in fact, pink is just plain cool.

Here's a quick tip: try to let go of all preconceived notions about colours. Human beings, from out of the womb all the way to their senior citizen years, can wear any colour they wish, and it should not attract judgement and/or imply any connection to gender.

Chapter 2: Gender-Bias in Toys and Marketing

When I was growing up, a few times per year my sister and I visited my Nan for the weekend. She used to take us to the local Kmart, and we were each allowed to choose one toy. The three of us would march straight to the pink-themed dolls, not bothering to browse the other aisles. I have red hair and freckles and always wondered why there wasn't a Barbie like me. But I didn't really care at the time. I had a blast dressing up this waif of a blonde bombshell in beach clothes. But what if I had gone straight to the trucks or the blocks? Or what if the dolls were marketed in blue packaging? Then would those conditioned to think blue was for boys be more open to their sons looking at dolls? Gender-bias in toys and marketing is a topic that is frequently mentioned by girls in STEM.

"In every store I have been to, the toy aisles have been divided into girl and boy aisles. The boy aisles consist of science kits and building sets, while the girl aisles consist of dolls and bracelet-making kits. This is very bothersome to me because it results in girls believing that they are not allowed to like the toys in the boy aisles. From a very young age, girls are discouraged from having STEM-related interests. My little sister is six years old, and I am very proud of her for what she is interested in. One of her favourite activities is building with LEGO. My little sister does not restrict herself solely to the pink girls' LEGO; she enjoys building the superhero and car LEGO sets, despite what her friends enjoy. This makes me very proud because it means that I have made an impact on her through my actions and decisions."

—Madison, Grade 11 student

While some toy stores have made small steps towards making change as far as colour divisions and gender-based set-up of their stores, marketing and promotional companies need to contribute and take a brave stand against gender stereotypes.

I was about ten when I became absolutely fanatical about *The A-Team* TV show. This American action-adventure series about a United States Army Special Forces unit featured four unique male characters who were on the run for a "crime they didn't commit." This show was targeted to boys; in fact, the only woman who appeared on the show regularly played a stereotypical character who needed to be rescued. But at the time, I didn't notice or care one iota. I thought everyone on the show was cool. They were brave and spontaneous and had crazy car chases! In fact, it was after watching *The A-Team* that I became interested in vehicles. So when I'd saved enough allowance to buy *The A-Team* figurines, you'd better believe I spent the extra bills on the signature black van to go with them. What did I do with that toy van? That van showed everyone in the neighbourhood what an awesome stunt driver I was. And what happened when the van crashed? I fixed it. Okay, so I didn't really fix it—but in my imagination, I changed tires, I repaired broken doors, and I got the engine running just in the nick of time. My point? Oddly enough, those *A-Team* toys inspired me to think differently—about what I could be and what I could do. Moreover, it was darn fun! I wonder what would've happened if I had started playing with trucks and tools earlier in my life? I hear from a lot of girls now in their teens who wish they'd had the opportunity to play with toys that were typically for boys. But most were taught to stay on the pink side of life.

"I grew up in an apartment with only my mom. I had a few toys but not very many. When I visited my friend's place, I really wanted to play with my friend's brother's trucks, but I knew that wouldn't be polite. I was just happy to play with any toys, so if they had to be dolls, that was okay. But I do wish I could've played with more trucks."

—Brianna, Grade 9 student

Brianna's commentary illustrates that beyond the realm of family beliefs, society itself has ingrained an overarching message in kids and adults alike that certain toys are for a particular gender. Sometimes it takes only one individual to convince a child it's okay to play with whatever toys he or she likes.

What can you do? Be that individual to encourage a child's imagination. Think outside the pink and blue toys. Let both boys and girls have the opportunity to explore, create, and imagine with different toys. And if anyone tells you otherwise, stand up for your approach. There's nothing wrong with, and in fact everything right about, a boy cuddling a doll—after all, don't we want our boys to grow up and be comfortable nurturing their own kids?

The gender-bias toy issue goes much beyond the product. Marketing plays a huge part when it comes to positioning and messaging. At the time of this publication there was an advertisement by an automotive company on TV that showed two women heading to a baby shower with a stereotypical pink cake for newborn "Taylor" (see chapter 1 for reference on colours). When they discover Taylor is not a girl but a boy, they deem themselves brilliant for being capable of getting a blue cake just in time for the shower. Talk about gender stereotyping marketed at a mass level. Think of how many people would've been involved in creating this ad in order for it to be produced, from story line to final product: a marketing department (or perhaps two: an internal one and an ad agency), management, filmmaker, producer, onsite assistants, actors, editors, and the list goes on. My point is, this script would've been read—and the footage would've been edited and seen—by numerous people. Did not even one person question playing into the pink vs. blue gender construct? An even better question is: did they not have a test group that included a diverse mix of parents watching the commercial for feedback?

Marketers and corporations need to take ownership of and accountability for product messaging. Companies have the opportunity to pleasantly surprise audiences with a fresh new perspective—in this case, a new standard of acceptance for baby shower cakes. However, the risk wasn't taken, and they remain among the humdrum droves whose mass messaging perpetuates gender bias. Along these same lines, corporations need to recognize that attracting women to their companies isn't simply about acquiring a different recruitment strategy; it's about changing culture and taking risks by using their influence to inspire a new way of thinking.

Chapter 3: The Power of Words

We've all seen it: cute frilly shirts for toddlers and young ones hung on the racks of the obviously branded girls' clothing sections that say, "I'm too pretty to do math" or "I only date heroes." The more we remain passive about this kind of messaging and the more our kids, and perhaps even we ourselves, gravitate towards this kind of branding, the less chance we will ever have at changing our culture. Why? Because when you have a cute-as-a-button walking billboard telling everybody that only boys are heroes and pretty girls don't do math, you help proliferate these stereotypes and they get all the more ingrained in people's heads. What can we do? First off, you and your family and friends can stay clear of this kind of clothing, and when you see it in stores, you can send the manager an email or letter to question the intentions of selling that kind of apparel. Don't ignore this stereotypical garbage that we've become immune to. This kind of clothing is impacting how society sees girls (and boys) and how girls see themselves.

Beyond offensive logos on T-shirts, the very way we speak can inadvertently perpetuate gender inequality. The use of the word "guys" has become so common, we don't even realize the frequency with which it's said. "Guys, let's get started"; "What do you guys think?"; "I need to talk to you guys for a minute" . . . For the most part, we have no ill intention when using "guys" in this way, but we don't have a widely used equivalent for women. The "guys" expression has been normalized and is now overused, but the fact is this term is not gender neutral.

Now you may be wondering if I'm getting too picky and morphing into silliness about word choice. But I once asked a younger student why she wasn't following the teacher's instructions and she said the teacher was only talking to the boys. I asked what exactly happened and she replied that the teacher had said, "Guys, start drawing your prototypes." Although this may seem like a trivial comment to some, clearly language and word choice has the risk of alienating others.

What can we do? Try to avoid using "guys" and instead use any one of the following as a replacement: everyone, everybody, class, team, students, people, etc. While I admit it's an extremely difficult habit to break, this is one change that is possible to make without causing complete upheaval in the system. Take it as a personal challenge to avoid using "guys" when addressing boys/men and girls/women.

Chapter 4: The Truth about Sports

*F*IRST Robotics Canada recently asked high school girls if they felt they missed opportunities because of being girls. Here's one standout message:

> "When I was young, I really wanted to learn karate. However, everyone was like, Karate is for boys. You should learn something more girly and feminine. Therefore, I learned piano instead of karate."

—Sidney, Grade 10 student

This type of comment was not uncommon. Unfortunately, the sports world is another victim of gender stereotyping and conditioning. If girls are encouraged to only try sports that have typically been popular with girls, such as dance, how will they ever fully know what they like and don't like? What about the boys? If boys only have the opportunity to play hockey, will they miss out on the chance to find their love of dance, or gymnastics, or what have you? The same goes for a "sport of the mind" such as robotics. If a girl is pushed away from doing such an activity or not exposed to it at all at a young age, there's no chance that she's going to get better at it or even try it. In the digital age, the more we can empower kids with technology, the more they will be prepared for our digital future. There are a few factors at play when getting girls involved in any kind of sport they haven't tried. They need to observe it; they need to feel it's okay to try it; and they need to be encouraged to practice it.

What can you do to help? Encourage girls to explore something new, even if society or cultural upbringing hasn't portrayed it as the norm. The only way to normalize the participation of girls in activities like robotics is to create an environment that is welcoming to girls and that they are comfortable in, and then position those girls as role models to attract more girls to the activity. Start a chain reaction of girls participating and supporting, and then get everyone involved: boys, girls, mentors, parents, everyone who supports.

Chapter 5: Career Choices

B oth girls and boys are interested in hearing about cool careers. Feedback from girls has shown us that we should focus on educating young people about not only STEM careers but also other jobs that may not be widely presented to and discussed with kids.

"We need young children to see that there are more careers than just engineer, doctor, lawyer, and teacher. Although these are amazing careers, there are only a certain number of jobs out there in these fields. There are so many other career options for these students to look into. Especially in STEM, there is software developer, data analyst, millwright, electrician, economist, technician, plumber, CNC machinist, and the list goes on. Students are told as soon as they go into high school that they need to choose a stream for their studies: Academic or Applied. When they hear this, they think, 'I am either going to take the smart student stream or the stupid student stream.' This needs to change because the education system is telling students at too young an age to choose their futures, and this defines where they go to school and therefore what careers they go into. If students were taught in ways conducive to their learning styles and informed of what possibilities lay ahead for their futures, we would have more people in general, including girls, in these lesser-known careers. I think this is especially important for girls because we are often sucked into traditional careers, and if we were aware of these other careers from a young age, then eventually we would not know what a 'traditional career' for women was; instead they would all just be careers for skilled people. We do not know what we do not know, so if we are not informed, then how will we know what is out there?"

—Jaeleen, *FIRST* Robotics Canada alumna & mentor

FIRST Robotics Canada, with the support of the government of Canada's CanCode program, recently published a mini-magazine in both digital and print formats that highlights careers and diverse role models in coding and programming. Resources such as this magazine are a great way to showcase opportunities in a visual format. And if you're an adult educating a young person about career options, take the time to learn about the diversity of jobs out there. Who knows what doors you may be opening? Finally, when discussing career options with young people, it's always important to include a perspective from someone who's been there, hence why role models are so important, as highlighted in chapter 16.

Chapter 6: Motivational Movies

Unfortunately, even in this day and age, we're still bombarded with messages and imagery that demonstrate that we haven't come very far when it comes to perceptions about the roles of women.

> "Hollywood doesn't portray First Nations women as strong and capable. In fact, I don't think there are any famous First Nations actresses in Hollywood. But I do know that any movies I've seen with women who are like me show them as only being the caregivers."
>
> —Anonymous, Grade 11 First Nations student

This comment is an excellent example of how gender isn't the only exclusionary factor when it comes to the expression of opportunities for women—race and ethnicity play huge parts as well. This stereotyping is a multi-level issue that requires diversity at the decision-making table to attempt to resolve it.

In the array of noise, there are a few movie gems waiting to be shared and enjoyed with both boys and girls. While everyone loves a good superhero movie, what if we redefined typical superheroes and took them to another level by including girls in STEM, courageous women from diverse backgrounds like indigenous communities, and underdog stories from underrepresented groups? For example, *Hidden Figures* is an excellent example of a movie that has the power to inspire people of all ages.

> "The first movie that I remember seeing that inspired me to be passionate about my love of STEM was *Hidden Figures*, the untold story behind three African-American scientists working at NASA in the 1960s. It did not hold back on showing the

realities that women in STEM went through. This movie illustrated to me that no matter what challenges you may face in your life or career, you must stand confidently as a brave and unapologetic woman of STEM. I was fourteen when I first saw the movie on opening night, and I know that I will never forget what that movie lit up inside me."

—Andrea, Grade 12 student

Here are a few more movies that reflect determination, inspiration, and the underdog story:

Akeelah and the Bee
The Gabby Douglas Story
Inside Out
He Named Me Malala
A Brave Heart: The Lizzie Velasquez Story
Dream Big: Engineering Our World

Recommendation: Check out amightygirl.com for a list of more movies and books that will inspire.

Chapter 7: Books to Spark Imagination

When I was growing up, my parents read books with me. I will forever cherish those special moments—hearing Mom or Dad act out characters, seeing their reactions when an exciting part of the story was revealed, and listening to the sounds of their voices speak the written words gave me feelings of belonging, comfort, and inspiration. Reading aloud together can turn bad days into good—the moment you get into a book, reality is momentarily forgotten. Suddenly you enter a world where anything is possible. Characters can do incredible things, and their personalities and adventures inspire kids to feel that they can do and be the same. In stories, you can build things out of random items and become a famous inventor, or rescue a flight of people by suddenly and magically knowing how to pilot a plane—anything can happen.

Learning how real-life heroes accomplished amazing feats also makes readers want to follow those footsteps. I love the series Little People, Big Dreams, which highlights famous women like Ada Lovelace, Rosa Parks, and Amelia Earhart. Targeted to ages five to eight, these picture books are an excellent way to introduce kids to renowned women who have made a huge impact on the world. Other books I like include

-*Baby Loves Aerospace Engineering* by Ruth Spiro

-*Wangari's Trees of Peace: A True Story from Africa* by Jeanette Winter

-*Velma Gratch and the Way Cool Butterfly* by Alan Madison and Kevin Hawkes

-*Maisy's Moon Landing: A Maisy First Science Book* by Lucy Cousins

-*Olga and the Smelly Thing from Nowhere* by Elise Gravel

All of these books inspire kids in some way: to be imaginative, to dream big, to think science is cool, and so much more. Reading with girls and boys is one avenue to opening young minds to a new world of possibilities.

Chapter 8: Science Is Fun Vs. Science Is Hard

M any girls say that they were always scared of science and math, as they believed these were hard subjects, and some also believed themselves to be less capable at them than boys.

> "My science class partner is a boy. I let him take the lead, as I'm pretty sure he's better in science than I am. Plus when the teacher talks to us, he always directs the conversation to him. But I do like science. I just don't think I'm good at it."
>
> —Alisha, Grade 11 student

Some people are better at science and math than others, just as some excel more in the arts. However, in general, society communicates that science is hard—especially for girls. This underlying message affects girls' approach to the subject, as they may doubt themselves before they even try. Instead of perceiving it as hard, what if everyone thought science was fun—like they do swings, parks, and balloons? In fact, we could link all of these fun things to science: swings with gravity, parks with ecology, and balloons to physics. And what if promotional visuals no longer portrayed the message that science is difficult? For example, LEGO and robotics programs are wonderful at getting kids talking about and interested in science. LEGO and robots are immediately perceived as fun, instead of hard. Sure, the more complex a robot becomes, the harder it looks to build; however, it's still a robot—which is perceived as fun overall. We need to change the messaging so that girls feel that science is fun and that they are capable of doing it— ultimately creating a welcoming space where they feel they belong. The same goes for coding: if we link coding to apps that appeal to girls, then that's going to change their approach to learning it. If a girl can create an app that feeds her pet fish at a certain time of day, or alerts her at the time when someone trespasses in her room—that's fun . . . and necessary! Science no longer has to be perceived as hard. With a focus on appealing visuals and messaging, it can be perceived as the most fun you'll ever have.

Chapter 9: Preteen Observations

As we observe girls and boys ages eight to twelve playing and working together, we see a difference in confidence, collaboration, and communication, compared to when they are teenagers. For the most part, younger girls in the preteen age group have not yet hit the stage where they begin to show signs of losing self-esteem. In contrast, we often see evidence of girls taking risks, speaking out, and working with boys as equal group members. We have a lot to learn from observing these boys and girls and how they work together. Sure, they can sometimes get frustrated with each other, but we as mentors have a greater opportunity at this age to curb any signs of disrespect by calling it out and changing the way kids treat each other. We need to do a better job of observing kids and seeing what they're doing, both right and wrong.

Once they get to their teens, there's more chance that self-confidence issues have already set in, peer pressure has become overwhelming and unbearable, and gender stereotyping is prominent and bothersome. What if we researched some amazing groups of preteen teams who have worked incredibly together and innovated beyond what people believed was possible? Think about the Classy Cyborgs, a *FIRST* LEGO League team that invented a Braille system and who went on to register a patent for it and garner extensive media attention for their ingenuity.

Lisa Andrade, former coach of the team and now a member of the *FIRST* Robotics Canada board of directors, noted an important point about girls and humanity. "Although this is a generalization, the girls seemed to have more empathy than the boys when trying to solve a problem for a particular demographic. For the Braille project, the girls understood on a deeper level the frustration, inequity, and isolation within the blind population. Because of this, it was the girls that brought the most innovative elements to the project idea, to address these needs." How can we make sure that these empathetic and innovative girls will not be pushed out of STEM? Clearly, these girls are difference-makers, and the world is missing out on their involvement in a discipline they often fail to explore as a result of bad experiences. What about the boys who show a lack of empathy? Is there a way to teach them to understand and feel empathy in a unique and effective manner? Or perhaps there is a way to position the boys who demonstrate a firm grasp of empathy as role models to their peers? It is our collective responsibility to make sure we are doing all we can to ensure that girls and boys stay in an industry they're passionate about, and to teach them how to work together effectively.

Chapter 10: Attitude Implications

Many *FIRST* Robotics Canada teams are paving the way for exemplary behavior and an inclusionary approach in STEM. Students are also finding ways to overcome barriers and stand out.

"I am half-Turkish, half-Iraqi, and I moved to Canada at the age of four. My mother and father were both raised in more modern areas of the Middle East with families that had reputations in the medical, engineering, and teaching fields; thus, I was raised to perform consistently and to the best of my abilities since childhood. Regardless of my upbringing in Canadian culture, I was verbally bullied a few times in elementary school due to my hijab and various Middle Eastern–related stereotypes. I took those moments as opportunities to reflect on how to more effectively portray my character so it does not get associated with my race or ethnicity, but rather with the type of person I am. I showed that I was a diligent student and always kept my behaviour in check to reverse stereotypes against me. In high school, I began to see that classmates and teachers had no great expectation from me in the beginning. I realized I had to build the expectation I wanted for myself once more. Similarly, on my *FIRST* team, there was no standard of work that was enforced on me due to my gender and race. I saw that as a perfect opportunity to show a high standard of work and create the expectation of passion in what I do. As the only female robot designer in my first year, I was learning and thus was never given deadlines to meet. I decided to show my initiative by finishing CAD [computer-aided drafting] drawings as they were being discussed, attending each meeting, and staying late working with the senior members. My team recognized my dedicated mindset and I was promoted to lead robot design in my second year."

—Anonymous, Grade 12 student

Not all students have the same attitude and opportunities as this student. Recurring feedback that I hear from girls on co-gender robotics teams is that they don't have the opportunity to take on a lead role like driver and/or that they are spoken down to by the male-dominant drive team members.

"The worst of the language that I've had to face as a leader in STEM was abusive words that almost escalated to physical violence. As bad as it sounds, my first idea when this happened was that I deserved it. Looking back, this was just about the worst thing I could have ever have thought in that moment. The words were harsh and cruel, such as 'You don't deserve this position' and 'If you were not a girl, I would have beaten you up by now.' As much as I would like to say that it was all a nightmare, I can say with certainty that this was not a bad dream. Language like this is horrendous and made me feel excluded from my second family: the STEM community."

—Andrea, Grade 12 robotics student

Why are some of the girls talked down to? Why is it assumed that talking down to them is okay, and why do other members of the group merely look on while it's happening? Throughout history, society has accepted leaders who treat people this way—whether the victims are women, underrepresented groups, or random underdogs. Somehow we've become immune to people treating each other in a condescending way to achieve a purpose. This is the way most conflicts have been won, lost, and battled—and in many ways, this condescending approach is still acceptable behaviour for leaders. Which brings me to a critical point: we have a chance to change the definition of a successful and equitable leader. What if the kids and youth of today created a new kind of leader whose approach embodies respect? A new leadership mantra that operates on inclusivity, strategy, and innovation? Sure, we are starting to see more women in leadership positions, but have we seen any shift in perceptions on what is acceptable behaviour and attitude as a leader? Indeed, this kind of shift would involve changing our culture at the deepest level, but if we started the culture shift at the preteen level, the culture could adapt as this generation evolved. What if we started a new leadership curriculum? It involves respectful competition but never at the expense of humanity. This is exactly why *FIRST* LEGO League Core Values should be taught in schools and communities around the world. Helping one another, working as a team, and honouring the spirit of friendly competition are the building blocks of this program and are the driving force behind shaping the mindsets of students. While not every team operates this way, the ideal situation is to get all students, teachers, mentors, and parents on board. We need to do a better job of shaping a new kind of leader that respects humanity. Let's try to learn what not to do from existing leaders who are breaking every rule of equality and kindness. Instead, let's write the new rules of respectful leadership.

As far as drive team leaders, they are the most visible players at robotics competitions. They are the ones spectators have the opportunity to observe closely—and if yelling and talking down to players is on display and accepted, this perpetuates the existing leadership mindset. What if we selected a few goal-accomplished, diverse drive team leaders to work collaboratively to change drive team culture? What if we paired them with the most influential and like-minded CEOs and stakeholders to brainstorm and execute a game plan for change and rally for a new and fresh approach to leadership? What if they were such strong personalities and voices that it started to shift mentalities in the world of youth as well as industry? What if they could redefine a leader? With a little effort and collaboration, they can.

Chapter 11: Overheard Conversations

Attitude is everything. Both boys and girls pick up on the attitudes of their parents, siblings, relatives, and friends towards pretty much anything they talk about. Parents' attitudes in particular make a huge difference to how sons and daughters view the world. If a father insinuates that his daughter is not as talented or as skilled as a boy, this will affect a girl's confidence. Conversely, if a daughter hears her mom say that girls can't be scientists, that will also greatly affect her attitude about herself and possibly affect her choices and potential. It's important to be keenly aware of what we say and who is listening. Just when we think there's no way a kid can hear what we're saying (after all, they're sitting in a soundproof room wearing headphones blasting music), we find out that indeed they've heard every single word and can repeat it verbatim. So we need to be aware of our own attitudes and words. Being self-aware as well as filtering some of our comments first by thinking twice about how they might sound to our kids are ways to avoid passing on our biases and stereotypes to young ones.

A teen girl once told me that she'd overheard her father telling his friend that there's no way she could excel in art since she's way too clumsy and lacks creative flare. While he wasn't trying to hurt her feelings, he did even more than that. After overhearing his comment, she stopped drawing and doing crafts—even though these activities gave her a creative outlet and she really enjoyed them. When I asked if her father knew she'd overheard this comment, she said no and, ironically, that she didn't want to hurt his feelings. It only takes one word, one sentence, one comment to affect a young girl's self-confidence, interest, and attitude, for the good and the bad. As mentors, we have to be keenly aware of this.

Chapter 12: Microaggression in Action

Examples of microaggression are everywhere and happen at every age. These are the everyday slights that undermine people and make them feel alienated—derogatory (yet often subtle) comments about someone's race, ethnicity, gender, physical ability, and so on are not only inappropriate but can be life-changing for the victims and for the people observing this behaviour. For teens, microaggression can be particularly tough to handle as negative comments can often be normalized and viewed as trivial. Even someone with the good intentions of sticking up for their peers may choose not to if the negative comments are not perceived by others as a big deal.

> "In order to help pave a way for girls in STEM, we need to help counteract microaggression in a respectable and effective way. You may wonder why this is important and think that we should instead focus on having girls speak up for themselves. Although that is important, in order to maintain a safe and fun environment, you need the members to help build each other up; you need all members to help counter and recognize microaggression so that others can feel that they are not alone."
>
> —Erica, Grade 12 student

Kids, youth, and adults need to learn how to pinpoint and counteract microaggression with what we call "microsponsorship." Microsponsorship is advocacy in the moment—standing up for others and recognizing inequalities when they happen. The more we can catch these normalized slights and pejorative language, the more we can support healthy mindsets about ourselves and others. Here are just a few examples of microaggression

- Interrupting someone when he/she repeatedly tries to share his/her thoughts

- Taking credit for an idea that isn't our own

- Verbal comments about physical traits, characteristics, talent, gender, etc.

Somehow many of us have become passive spectators of microaggression, letting it happen without even trying to call it out or doing the right thing. Although it can be a fearful thing to do, you can counter this aggression with sponsorship. You can stand up for the victim just by drawing attention—in a calm and polite manner—to what you've seen or heard. For example, if you see someone repeatedly interrupted, recognize it in the moment: "I just noticed that Emelia was trying to say something. Emelia, what were you going to say?" And as far as someone taking credit for someone else's idea, you could respond with the following: "Thanks for the comment, James. I remember Maddie offering that idea at last week's meeting. I think we all agree we should move forward with it! Thanks for thinking of it, Maddie." If that approach scares you, you're not alone. Most people would rather not do or say anything about ill behaviour if mentioning it will cause tension in a group.

Practicing microsponsorship is one of the bravest things you can do. Try to approach it like fighting crime. You're preventing future hurt and harmful conditions to others just by calling out this behaviour—one perpetrator at a time. Perhaps the microaggressor isn't even aware of the impact of his or her comments, or maybe they are aware and don't care. Either way, if you were the victim in the situation, surely you would hope that someone would jump in and help you.

A girl participating in a STEM-related activity, like a robotics team, may be driven out of the team or club (or industry) entirely if microaggression continues. It is even harder to handle when it's directed by an adult at a student or child. At times, this situation can seem somewhat hopeless for students if they feel powerless to change attitudes or aren't brave enough to stick up to their mentors, teachers, and parents. This is why when we, as adults, witness this type of behaviour from our peers, we must find a way to speak up. Whether that's by talking to that perpetrator privately or finding a way to speak up in the moment, it has to be done. If we fail to do so, our ignorance of that behaviour will result in kids and youth modelling that same ignorance, or even worse, being the perpetrators of that behaviour. Educate yourself on microaggression, recognize it in the moment, and counteract it with microsponsorship. Microaggression can be the root cause of hostile environments and hatred, and it does not provide space for growth and opportunity—in fact, it's pushing people out of certain industries for good.

Chapter 13: Codes of Conduct

All organizations, clubs, camps, and activities should have a code of conduct in place and accessible to all. This may sound like common sense, but it actually isn't always the case. The code of conduct needs to be available for everyone to see, and it needs to be easy to reference and share. Gone are the days when a printout was the best method. The document should be online and, most importantly, not buried within the mice type at the footer of the site. Organizations need to take greater responsibility to prevent worst-case scenarios that involve the following issues:

• Bullying

• Sexual harassment

• Inappropriate behaviour and language

• Microaggression

• Lewd commentary and miscellaneous shenanigans

It's critical that kids of all ages and their parents know the details of and agree to the code of conduct before participating in an organization or activity. The code should not be written in vague or elusive language—it should be as explicit as possible so that there's no chance for a perpetrator after a misdeed to profess ignorance that the inappropriate action was addressed. Leave no stone unturned when it comes to explanation of what is acceptable and unacceptable behaviour. Own your code, be proud of it, and share it widely. The more vocal you can be about it, the more awareness you'll raise that there's zero tolerance for behaviour that doesn't adhere to it. Spell it out, communicate it, and then stand by it.

Chapter 14: The Importance of Self-Talk

I t's not just the folks who surround us who lift us up or bring us down. Ultimately it's the messages we communicate to ourselves that will determine a healthy state of mind. Throughout my life, I've struggled with my weight. At one of my worst points, I was forty-five pounds overweight. As I am five foot one, this extra weight had an extremely detrimental effect on me. Not only did I physically feel like crap, I had zero respect for myself. Sure, every once in a while I could muster up a compliment to myself (that was usually related to me being a fat girl with a sense of humour), but most of the time, I tried to keep my mind busy so I didn't become obsessed with degrading self-talk. I was convinced I was not worthy of anything good in my life. When you're down on yourself, it's pretty tough to follow a positive self-talk mantra. But if you can make a conscious effort to do it, even during the lowest of the low times, it will change your life for good. Positive internal communication can stop you from diving into a hole of darkness or a wave of depression; it can help refocus your mind to hopeful thoughts.

For me, there have been times when I've had to limit social media scrolling. If I focus on all of the amazing things certain people are doing, I end up comparing myself to others and their lives. Social media has become a psychological demon for some of us, as comparisons can be inevitable. As New York Times–bestselling author Pastor Steve Furtick once said, "The reason we struggle with insecurity is because we compare our behind-the-scenes with everyone else's highlight reel." If we focus on the amazing lives that others are living or take less pride in our own, it will be even harder to bounce back from feelings of negativity. If you have to, ban yourself from social media for a few days, or for however long it takes—at least until you've had time to self-talk your way back to feeling that you are worthy of happiness and gratitude for your life and story, regardless of how many likes your posts get online.

Girls and women in STEM have a powerful friend in self-talk. Women who waver in confidence about their talent, skills, and competency in STEM can overcome the situation by strategies including self-talk. I admit it's difficult to use positive self-talk on demand, but if you can harness its power and do just that, it's yet another resource to add to your creative resilience toolbox. Sometimes you can even anticipate how you're going to feel before a challenging situation has happened. In this case, you can practice the self-talk line you will use on yourself. For example: "They don't realize I'm brilliant in CAD. I'm really good at doing CAD, and I'm going to show them all what I can do. I'm even going to strive for the design lead role next season."

Self-talk your way to unwavering self-confidence and success. Whoever is on your support team (parents, mentors, friends, teachers) also has a responsibility to remind you that self-talk and confidence-building is crucial to your self-worth and personal growth.

Chapter 15: Question Period Priority

General Motors Canada invited me to attend an empowerment event for employees. One of the panellists, referring to her own experience as an engineer, commented that asking questions was undoubtedly one of the keys to her success and ability to move forward in her STEM career. Many high school girls have confided in me that they are often too nervous to ask questions. They believe that they are the only "stupid" person in the bunch, so why would they ask a question in front of everyone at risk of being ridiculed? We need to do a better job of creating environments where curiosity and questions are okay—in fact, where they are encouraged. Whether you're a part of a robotics club or a boardroom meeting, if somebody asks a question, express your appreciation to them for asking it. Sometimes this is all it takes to encourage a culture of open communication. If you're in an environment where a question is asked, no matter by whom, and you hear snickering or rude jokes and/or witness yawns or rolls of the eyes, it is your job—everyone's job—to practice microsponsorship. For example, a supportive comment following the question could be: "I was wondering the same thing, Becca. I'm glad you asked that." Or you could say something like, "Excellent question, Mara. It made me think of another related question."

Boys and girls will refrain from asking questions if they are not in an open and safe environment to do so. What that means is that we are missing out on opportunities to discuss and clarify topics in further detail. Especially in matters related to STEM, students must ask questions in order to fully comprehend, critically analyze, and then apply an innovative mindset to the topics at hand. Asking questions is one key to survival in a STEM career. If you're an instructor or mentor, take as many opportunities as possible to solicit questions. Try to encourage everyone to participate, making clear it's a judgement-free zone. Give the necessary pauses so that students have the time to consider their inquiries, and moreover approach question period in a manner that lets everyone feel it's okay to ask.

Chapter 16: The Reality of Role Models

B esides observing role models in books and movies, it's vital for girls to see people like them succeed in a myriad of industries—particularly in STEM fields.

> "Half the girls I talk to like math, science, and engineering, but they've never had any role models push them to pursue those careers. So they follow their peers into careers that are more traditionally adopted by women, and more socially acceptable. The more we can educate these girls and expose them to the masses who are already excelling in their respective fields, the more I think we can help women make better-informed decisions."
>
> —Thuvishan, *FIRST* Robotics Competition alumnus and mentor (male)

There's a level of comfort knowing that an inspiring woman is thriving in whatever industry she has chosen. They say "if she can see her, she can be her." This is absolutely true, and it's crucial that we include diverse role models to inspire all.

> "I'm mixed race: black, Middle Eastern, Hispanic, and Moroccan. It's a sad reality that I say that it's lucky I don't look black. In the field I'm going into (computing occupations), between 1 and 3 percent of groups represented are black women. As a result of that and other subconscious racial biases, black women are at a huge disadvantage when it comes to things like job interviews."
>
> —Kouthar, University student and mentor

This situation has to change. At *FIRST* Robotics Canada, we're creating various initiatives to encourage all girls to explore and succeed in STEM. These initiatives are strengthened by the participation of experts in the community and difference-makers such as Cherryl Lewis, who is the executive director of the African Canadian Christian Network (ACCN). Cherryl and ACCN formed Canada's first community black youth robotics team created to nurture black youth's pursuit of STEM careers, and to demonstrate to them that they have what it takes to be at the STEM table. With this undertaking, Cherryl is clearly making a change. But it's critical that all girls see that STEM is an industry where they belong—hence the need for role models.

We need peer role models, senior-level role models, professional role models, and celebrity role models. Ideally, a role model structure incorporating these four levels of inspiration will help girls face adversities, stay in their chosen industry, and thrive in their fields. For a look at the influence of a peer role model, let's take, for example, a girl at the *FIRST* LEGO League level (ages nine to fourteen). She needs to see other girls her age happily participating on a robotics team so she can better imagine herself doing the same thing. A peer role model can show her the ropes, whether through direct mentorship or observation, and can make her feel more comfortable and confident about being a part of the endeavour.

One level up from a peer role model is a senior role model, perhaps a high school student mentoring an elementary school student. The greater experience and age of the high school student allows her role to serve a slightly different purpose than that of a peer. A senior role model can offer advice and insight with a been-there-done-that approach, as opposed to a peer role model, who also serves as a companion and in some cases a friend. The mentorship from senior role models can drive girls to push further and explore new pursuits in order to be like them.

Up next, professional role models. These can exist for any age group, but the level of impact significantly increases during and after high school, when girls are considering their future journeys more seriously, and when they're looking for signs and connections that will help them choose a career path. If young girls have never met, seen, talked to, or heard of a woman engineer in manufacturing, it's less likely they will follow that career path—let alone even know that job exists! That's why visits to schools and communities from industry professionals are key to young people learning about what kinds of opportunities exist for them.

Take, for instance, Vanessa Vakharia, otherwise known as The Math Guru. Vanessa runs a boutique math and science tutoring school in Toronto, and she also visits schools, is featured on media, and talks to kids and youth about math. One interaction with Vanessa and you'll be convinced that math is cool: she's a math wiz, a rock star, and most definitely a STEM role model. Students interacting with Vanessa are going to be inspired and get a different (more positive) point of view about math. Professional role models can simply inspire by being seen and sharing their stories; the relationship kids have with them does not have to be frequent or defined. This is why it's increasingly vital for kids and youth organizations to be the conduits for these types of opportunities. Take Dr. Eugenia Duodu, the CEO of Visions of Science Network for Learning. She calls herself "the unlikely scientist" because, being a black woman in STEM, she had to undertake a courageous journey to arrive at where she is today. Eugenia spoke at the Girls in *FIRST* Weekend and the feedback we received after her brief talk was overwhelmingly positive. Here are a few choice quotes from three 2018 Girls in *FIRST* Weekend participants:

> "Dr. Eugenia Duodu was the most thought-provoking speaker to me and was relatable even though we are many years apart. When she told the story of when she went to speak at an elementary school and the kids insisted she did not resemble a scientist, it resonated with me. I also faced criticism in the same sense because I was not seen as an appropriate leader for a robotics team. The way Eugenia spoke about how she overcame these assumptions to become such a strong leader was very touching and something that I feel many of us needed."

"Dr. Eugenia really inspired me. I like how she talked about inclusion in the science field and how she pushed through the difficult parts of her schooling and her work. It inspired me when she talked about how everything will be hard if you really want to succeed."

"Dr. Eugenia inspired me because I can relate to many of the obstacles she is facing both as a woman and racially. She inspired me to keep moving forward and emphasized that those who try and bring you down should have the tiniest effect on your life and progress."

Other role models who have an impact are celebrities. Celebrity role models are those famous for what they do in an industry. Scientist and science-television host Dr. Jennifer Gardy inspires young women by her love of, and enthusiasm for, science. I had the opportunity to interview Dr. Gardy when I wrote an article about germs and microbes for *OWL Magazine*. I never imagined that viruses, bacteria, fungi, and parasites could be so fascinating! And the most inspiring part about it? Kids felt the same. Readers (ages nine to thirteen) thought that learning about germs with Dr. Gardy was so cool! She is a celebrity role model whom young girls aspire to be. It doesn't matter that most girls will most likely never meet her in person; her passion and reputation for being a super cool disease detective inspires them.

One prime example of global celebrity role models are the all-girls robotics team members from Afghanistan, who were themselves inspired by entrepreneur and innovator Roya Mahboob. These girls defied all odds to compete in a robotics competition in the US after getting denied entry multiple times, and they are influencing people all over the world by showing that the impossible can be possible, and to never give up.

There are so many other celebrity STEM role models out there—we just don't hear them talked about as much as pop culture celebrities. Who knows, maybe one day we'll be discussing the latest STEM-celebrity role model instead of gossiping about who's divorcing whom in Hollywood.

Chapter 17: STEM and STEAM

Years ago when STEM started to get traction as an educational framework, the "A" was never part of the acronym. To many, science, technology, engineering, and math stood alone and apart from the arts with regards to preparing the young leaders of tomorrow. However, creativity is ingrained in STEM; in order for STEM fields to exist and evolve, creative thought is a must. The arts have always been a part of STEM—in the design of an invention, the creative workings of the latest technological gadget, and the marketing plans for a STEM prototype, for example. It wasn't long before the entire STEM movement was shifting to include the buzz-worthy A. The arts and, along with them, creativity are absolutely vital in all *FIRST* Robotics programs. For girls who may feel more comfortable with the arts, knowing there's a creative task that they can contribute to may be enough of a pull to get them interested in knowing more. From that point on, although the arts elements may have been the hook, these girls feel like they belong, so they may be more open to exploring science and technology. Once they feel a sense of acceptance, they'll then have a safe place in which to explore STEM.

The danger with letting girls gravitate towards, and stay involved in, only the artistic tasks on the team is that they may never want to take a risk and try another role. In fact, the same goes with the boys. If the boys love the technical side of the build, it may be difficult, and seemingly counterintuitive, to ask them to focus on the marketing and presenting. However, diversifying everyone's roles and tasks gives students a chance to try different facets of the team so that they can ultimately decide what aspects are of interest to them. In general, girls have proven to have excellent time management, marketing, and communication skills, hence why many girls end up in these roles on their respective robotics teams and in future careers. However, many have also expressed to me that they want to expand beyond these roles and try driving, building, and experiencing the technical side of the robots. Some robotics teams are so focused on students staying in silos and subcommittees (for various reasons, including sticking to their perceived recipe to win), the girls often don't have a chance to try other roles.

> "I would try to implement that for all students on a robotics team, they must be assigned both a technical task (in terms of design, building, and testing of the robot) and a more soft-skill task (awards, outreach, community involvement); that way both girls and boys are given equal opportunities for all types of tasks on the team. Then all students receive the hands-on, learn-to-use-tools experience, and everyone learns how to speak professionally with people."

> —Mikaela, *FIRST* Robotics Competition alumna and mentor

It is in the task delegation stage at which the mentors have to ensure they create and maintain the type of environment that is accepting of others trying—and failing—in other roles than just sticking to the one they are good at and/or accustomed to. This goes for boys as well as girls. I know amazingly talented and artistic boys on robotics teams who have stayed on the technical side, as that was the path recommended to them.

> "I saw the girls on my team working on a really cool robotics game for kids that incorporated graphic design and illustration. I wanted to join that sub-group, but no boy had never participated in art projects on the team, so I stayed out of the way. I had some really cool ideas for it, though."

> —Simon, Grade 11 student

Bottom line? Regardless of what acronym you use, STEM or STEAM, emphasize the importance of the arts and creativity. Always be cognizant that all team members should have an opportunity to try new roles and tasks in a safe environment.

Chapter 18: Exploration Is Better than Perfection

Many girls have a tendency to strive for perfection. Girls Who Code founder Reshma Saujani said we need to start focusing on bravery over perfection. According to Reshma, "we raise our girls to be perfect, and our boys to be brave." Reshma's TED Talk is a breath of inspiration and a classic commentary on perfection.

Whether a girl has grown up feeling pressure to avoid failure or has experienced a devastating tribulation that broke down her confidence level, she may live her life trying to be perfect. This mentality can be seen in girls who choose not to try new experiences and those who find themselves in a complete frenzy in anticipation of an important task. The drive for perfection is holding many people back—especially girls. Girls are choosing not to put their best foot forward as they're terrified they will fail, and therefore not be perfect. Some girls are preoccupied with this idea because they believe that being so-called perfect is what others want to see. Essentially they're pleasing others and sacrificing self-discovery. This fixation might be most obvious when kids are in their teens, but it creeps in long before that age. Even little girls may try way too hard to please people, as they think that makes others happy.

I personally experienced the struggle to be perfect after I was diagnosed with type 1 diabetes at the age of nine. Health professionals back then tended to use language to condition patients to behave in certain ways. Communication strategies were used that drew a clear line between the "good" and the "bad" patients. The good were those who stuck to their healthy diet, checked their blood sugar multiple times per day, and obtained a "normal" HbA1C result (a test that indicated your blood sugar level for the past three months). If this A1C was high, you were conditioned to feel you were bad. I desperately wanted to be a good girl. I tried so hard to do everything I was supposed to in order to achieve an A1C that I felt made the doctors and everyone proud. The problem? It was impossible to be perfect all of the time. And striving for it resulted in negative side effects—like feeling stressed, getting upset when I felt I couldn't try any harder, and most of all, worrying that I'd disappointed people. I went to a clinic every three to six months to have my results monitored, and regardless of how hard I tried, sometimes life got in the way. Up until I graduated high school, I pretty much aimed to be perfect when it came to my A1C, and everything else for that matter.

Now as I look back, I realize my struggle for perfection made it impossible for me to ever feel satisfied with any of my accomplishments and was damaging to my self-esteem. Sometimes when we try hard at something but perceive those results as poor or bad, it can cause us to crack. Meaning it can cause an absolute breakdown . . . and I've had my fair share of those as well! Trying to be perfect is dangerous. Recognize it in yourself and try to help others when you see they're putting unnecessary and unrealistic pressure on themselves. Mental health–wise, we will all be the better for it.

For mentors, parents, coworkers, bosses, and a host of other influencers, always remember this mantra: let her try. Whether she's a schoolgirl attempting to build her first robot, a teen who's curious about using a drill press, or a full-grown woman who would like to learn how to change a tire—let her try. I repeat: Let. Her. Try. It may sound ridiculously simple, but the number of girls who report they do not have the opportunity to try a new task is astounding. While it might take time and patience from the mentor when letting a protégé attempt something she hasn't done before, the mentor's support may have an impact on that girl's entire life. While it can test the patience of the mentor to see the participant in action fumbling with the task at hand, a girl needs the chance to fail in order to succeed. This is the only way she is going to learn.

"I have a natural talent for programming, but when it comes to understanding the engineering of our robot, it takes me a long time and a lot of hard work, while there're a couple of friends of mine who instantly understand it. But after my mentor sat down with me for a couple of hours and explained everything to me, I felt a lot better and understood a lot more. That's an example of what a mentor or educator has to do!"

—Rohma, Grade 10 student

It's also important to remember to always avoid any sort of sarcastic humour about a girl's performance of that task, as it may cause her to feel bad and incompetent. I can't even count the number of times that I either turned down a never-attempted-before task or stopped mid-task as I was afraid I was going to look and feel stupid. In my personal experience, patient and encouraging mentors are rare. Be one of those extraordinary teachers with the kind of patience that results in a girl being proud of what she just learned and accomplished, no matter what it took to get there.

Chapter 19: Support Networks, Male Champions, and Allies

Women can be critical and judgmental of each other. This is quite an absurd phenomenon since we're all fighting for equality, happiness, and the chance to share our voice. But for some reason, some women tend to judge each other—especially when it comes to people they are jealous of. For whatever reason, we need to change this judgmental mindset immediately. If we want to create a more inclusive environment, we have to support each other—even if it's opposite to what our mindset tells us. Jealousy can tear us apart, and if we let it take over, we may not like who we become or how we behave. So how do we handle jealousy so that it doesn't overwhelm us? Always, always try and see the good in people, even when all you first see is negativity. Remember, that person you're jealous of has weaknesses and downfalls and is also not perfect. Maybe that person is dealing with unimaginable struggles at home or at school or in their head. Counteracting jealousy with empathy can go a long way to building relationships. Girls in STEM need to support other girls in STEM. These are the connections that are going to get us through the hard times. Turn that jealousy into empathy. Kindness rules all. We are our own allies.

Male champions for change are also a huge support for women. These men are allies who have a heightened awareness of the way in which others are treated, and that makes them powerful leaders and changemakers—as well as better team players. This empathy allows them to be more open-minded to learning about gender equality and to have more drive to become contributing members of the community. These leaders realize the importance and impact of gender equality and being role models for other men. They also acknowledge that gender equality is a win-win situation for them, as collaboration leads to innovation, profitability, and a happier team.

"In this day and age, men and women are equals,
and there are many men that are just as aware of this
as women. One example of this are the male
champions of STEM. These are the men in STEM
fields who are supporters of the advancement in the
inclusion of women in STEM. When these male
champions are introduced to people who believe
that women are not as capable as men, they are able
to express their positive opinions on the subject.
This will give those with negative opinions a male
with a different perspective who they may listen to
more."

—Madison, Grade 11 student

Besides my father, who has been the biggest male influence in my life, there are a number of other men that I consider my male champions. Mark Breadner, president of *FIRST* Robotics Canada, has been a huge support in many ways, and has particularly helped me build more courage in order to take risks. If Mark hadn't believed in my talent and abilities as an employee and a person, I wouldn't have had the opportunity to grow as I have, both personally and professionally.

Another male champion for me is Paul Rietdyk, who is the vice president of engineering, construction, and storage and transmission operations at Union Gas Limited. I've got to know Paul from collaborations at *FIRST* Robotics Canada and have the utmost respect for his approach, demeanor, and ability to get things done in a quiet way. He never takes over a room in conversation, but when he says something, it's always worth listening to.

When I was invited to meet a male-dominated high school robotics team, I had doubts about how I would be received by the boys and males in the room, as the topic was diversity and inclusivity. A few weeks prior to the visit, I was struck by the idea to invite Paul to join me for my presentation. As a member of the *FIRST* Robotics Canada Executive Advisory Board, Paul graciously agreed. We both planned our parts—mine coming first in the presentation order. The room was full of male mentors and teenaged boys (minus a few women and a handful of girls).

The audience was cold. Stark cold. The crowd gawked blankly at me during my introduction and then further into my presentation, and my words about diversity and inclusion got completely ignored, despite my creative attempts at keeping everyone's attention. It was hard to focus when I literally witnessed yawns, chatter, and even a roll of the eyes. As I went through my well-practiced spiel, my spirits slowly deflated. At that moment, I honestly felt like nobody in the world cared about what I was talking about. If I had been onstage by myself, this presentation may have come to a devastating close—I can picture a ringleader in a top hat pulling me offstage with the notorious hook. But that's not what happened. I had Paul by my side. And when it was his turn to present, he commented on some of the insights I had offered and brought me and my thoughts back into the conversation. As Paul spoke, I could slowly feel my deflated spirits inching back to normal size. And the more he expressed that he believed in what I was saying, the more I could feel the audience giving credence to my presentation. Sure, it was maddening that the men instantly paid attention to him, despite the fact that they had ignored me entirely. But that anger was blanketed by the powerful boost from a male champion. He believed in me, and what I said, and so us presenting in tandem was a perfect way to get our messages across in a respectful way. I will never forget the mix of emotions I had that day. On one hand, I felt the true barriers some girls in STEM face. But on the other hand, I had a male champion by my side who helped amplify what I was saying so that my message got through. The more girls and boys, and women and men, can become partners and lift each other up, the more we can garner the attention of everyone in the room.

Mark Hardy, vice president at SYNNEX Canada, has also been a huge champion for me. Even when I was just starting out at *FIRST*, I always felt that Mark respected the work I do. He's a hard worker and has established an amazing network of people he can mobilize at any time to get involved in various initiatives. Once we both understood that we were on the same page as far as work ethic, the sky was the limit on our collaborative potential. He's been kind enough to introduce me to his many connections and to suggest ways in which I can work with them. He also pushes me to see beyond the busy every day, and has invited me to women in technology events that have opened doors to many opportunities. In addition, Mark is one to tell things as they are. It's critical to remember that when someone is kind enough to offer you constructive criticism (man or woman), you can take it, and even probe for more—no matter how disappointed you may be to hear it at first. This is the kind of honest feedback that is often hard to obtain and could be a game changer for your professional development.

We could all benefit from male champions who can help us dream bigger. They can push us to do more and open our eyes to a new way of seeing—because they haven't faced the same barriers as we have, so they can offer a new perspective. Perhaps you don't believe you have male champions in your life, but look around. Is there someone who has always stuck up for you? Someone who listens intently when you talk? Someone who offers you advice and insight? Maybe that person is a male champion.

The more we recognize the impact and potential of male champions, the more quickly we can work towards collaborative innovation and helping underrepresented groups be heard in this world. For high school girls, you can find male champions in your peers. Having a good rapport with boys who treat you as equals will give you a greater understanding of the male approach and mindset. What if high schools all had to assign boy and girl champions to each other? What if they had to agree that no matter what, each person had to stick up for and support their partner? A champion's role is to help support you and further your goals. If we all had a dedicated champion that we were loyal to, imagine how that structure might change clichés? And mental health issues? And bullying? What if your champion recognized your positive qualities and shared them with others? What if you did the same for him or her? This kind of relationship could lead to a stronger understanding of each other and also further prepare youth for today's workforce and the reality of working closely with, and sticking up for, each other in a professional milieu. Do you have the courage to consider working with a male champion? Is the champion brave enough to be your powerful ally?

Chapter 20: Boardroom Banter and Job Interviews

R esearch has shown that most women will not apply to a job they don't feel they are fully qualified for, which is a big contrast to men, who take risks and apply regardless of whether they're missing some must-have skills listed in the description. What does that mean? It means that women take their job postings very literally and seriously. In other words, women take the verbiage as absolute—therefore possibly missing out on opportunities because they don't take the risk and apply. In this situation, ideally women could build up the courage to apply to jobs they're interested in, even when they feel their competition may be much more deserving or qualified than they are. But what else can be done? Human resource professionals, writers of job postings, and recruiters can consider the implications of wording. Consider the following:

•   Does the posting indicate that there's no flexibility in the qualifications needed?

•   Does it sound like the company is stringent on the criteria?

•   Does the job description conjure up an image of the perfect candidate or the ideal candidate?

Often despite a job description that lists must-have skills, the company will still accept candidates who don't have those qualifications—but sadly many women will have been fooled into thinking they aren't qualified enough to apply. What we should do as job providers or HR professionals is this: if a must-have is actually a nice-to-have, then list it that way. If communication skills far outweigh other skills, come right out and say it.

Job searchers are often in a vulnerable position. Sure, there are the fortunate ones who are looking for a job while they're employed, but many are not in that position and they may be risk-averse. If the wording in a job posting is too specific and thus it's going to reduce the quality of your candidate pool, then you may want to rethink your communication strategy, and figure out how to change it. Are there other women in the company in that particular role? If so, ask them their opinion on the posting and be completely open to their feedback and suggested changes. Something as simple as paying close attention to wording could be a step to your company gaining more employees from diverse backgrounds.

"A workforce with diversity of thought is critical to meeting the toughest challenges facing our society. Research has shown that gendered language has no impact on men's decisions to apply to postings but may dissuade women. Words such as strong, direct, and competitive are viewed as masculine and could prevent a qualified woman from applying. Many companies have recognized this fact and are altering the language in their job postings to make roles gender neutral.

As a female engineer working in a historically male-dominated profession, I was not initially aware of the impact words could have on attracting female talent. It was through my involvement in our STEM outreach committee and Women's Council affinity group, in addition to working with the talent acquisition team that I had the opportunity to talk to more women and gain a different perspective and context. After reflection, I realized that I, too, had not applied to positions specifically because I felt I did not fit. I'm proud that the team at General Motors has adopted gender-neutral language in our job postings to ensure we attract the industry's best talent."

—Regan Dixon, engineering group manager at General Motors Canada

Another matter to look at is whether there is only one person doing one-on-one interviews at your company and who ultimately decides who goes on to the next level of the interview stage. If this is the case, you will want to seriously rethink your interview strategy. An equal number of women and men on an interview panel will support the vision that your STEM-related company has to hire and retain women employees. Both men and women on an interview panel should be allocated an equal number of questions and given the same talking time to connect with the candidate. Having at least two people, preferably more, participate in an interview panel will offer you different perspectives, and unconscious bias is less likely to cloud the final decision.

Once young women enter the workforce, they can have issues adjusting to certain workplace cultures. *FIRST* Robotics Canada program alumni have a leg up on coping with this challenge as they've learned teamwork strategies, creative resilience, and communication techniques. But there'll still be experiences that may be completely foreign to them. For example, in some male-dominated boardrooms, the pre-meeting banter consists of sports, sports, and more sports. Sure, some women like to talk about sports, but since women are not a large part of national competitive sports broadcasts on mainstream television, it's not as common for them to be fans the way men are. Don't get me wrong, I'm an NFL fan and have engaged in in-depth discussions about Peyton Manning emerging from retirement, training techniques from the legendary Jerry Rice, and the absurdity of Rob Gronkowski's hard hits. But sports does tend to be a more male-centric arena. So when the boardroom banter begins about the latest open-ice hit at a hockey game, consider raising other topics to get all participants engaged—such as industry trends, news, or family. These are topics that span gender divides. Turn your radar on to detect if a certain conversation is alienating people in the room. Make it your job to bring quiet bystanders into the conversation or change the topic entirely. Warming up with casual conversation is always a nice icebreaker before launching into serious business. Why not take advantage of that opportunity and get everyone involved so that by the time the meeting starts, participants already feel like they belong in the group?

Chapter 21: EDI and Bystander Training

Who should take EDI (equity, diversity, and inclusion) and bystander training? Everyone: students, teachers, professors, CEOs, managers, anyone who works with people . . . which is, as I said, everyone. EDI training consists of education about implicit bias and unconscious bias, as well as equity, diversity, and inclusivity issues at school, in the workplace, and in communities. Bystander training inspires a culture of respect by recognizing the power of bystanders to help others in their time of need—promoting the community responsibility approach. But why does this training matter? Many of us live in insular worlds where understanding the experiences of others beyond our own community can be challenging. Being mindful of how we think of and treat others, as well as becoming more self-aware, can benefit us all professionally and personally—we may even become better people for it.

EDI training programs are becoming more prevalent. One example is *FIRST*'s collaboration with the National Alliance for Partnerships in Equity (NAPE) to develop training for coaches, mentors, volunteers, partners, and stakeholders who work with students to enable them to create diverse, inclusive, and equitable teams. The three-part training module course available at firstinspires.org was prepared for the *FIRST* community, but the content and situations can be applicable to other environments.

An organization called Project Implicit launched an Implicit Association Test (IAT) that can effectively be used to generate conversation, and open eyes to self-understanding. The IAT was created to deliver insight into implicit attitudes and beliefs that people either hide or are not fully aware of existing.

Word of caution. Since the EDI buzz took off a mere few years ago, you now see an increase in diversity trainers, conferences, and consultants who want to make you and your company EDI-ready for the future. If you hire one of these services or consultants, do your research and be sure that these so-called experts are qualified to teach you and your team about this topic. With some corporations scrambling to catch up on the EDI front, desperation to demonstrate action can result in poor choices for EDI counsel.

Bystander training is also important to help raise awareness and mobilize the community to take action when witnessing a potential act of abuse and violence. The Canada Safety Council outlines how everyone can help when it comes to public safety and harnessing their power as bystanders. The more we acknowledge the "bystander effect" of public citizens turning a blind eye to someone in trouble, the more we can be alert citizens who will be active participants when someone is in need.

Chapter 22: Councils, Conferences, and Motivational Speakers

T he lack of women in the STEM industry has resulted in a multitude of councils and committees created for the purpose of making change. The issue with many of these councils is that they are composed solely of women. When I approached Dr. Imogen Coe about joining *FIRST* Robotics Canada's Girls in STEM Executive Advisory Council, she told me in no uncertain terms that my mistake was forming an all-women's council. From that point forward, I approached committees and councils in a different way: diversity in membership is the only way we are going to get to real ideas and solutions. This is why the Girls in STEM Executive Advisory Council is now composed of both men and women, and why the Girls in STEM Student Council will evolve to include boys as well.

"In the past, women were not allowed to join a lot of stuff the men were in. In the present, we have a lot of things that are just for women. For example, girls' robotics teams, conferences, and clubs. Is this not doing the same thing as men used to do to us? I believe that in order for women to truly be treated as equals, they cannot exclude men from their groups. Women and men will never truly be equal, it is physically impossible; however, the way we are treated, paid, and respected can be equal. Men and women can accomplish so much more when they work together. Men and women have different types of brains, we think about problems differently, and we come up with different solutions. However, if we put those differences together, we will come up with a much better solution because there was collaboration of two different ways of thinking and approaching the problem. To break the barrier, we need to stop creating a new one."

—Jaeleen, *FIRST* Robotics Competition alumna & mentor

When we think of women's groups fighting for equality, we tend to only think of women participants. It's interesting to note that male-based councils fighting for equality have been around for almost a decade in countries like Australia. In 2010, Australia's appointed Sex Discrimination Commissioner established a Male Champions of Change initiative. This strategy supports male leaders in engaging and welcoming more women in leadership roles in Australian companies, government, and society. Another organization, Men Advocating Real Change (MARC), is committed to achieving gender equality in the workplace through the support of men. We all can learn from these organizations by finding out the kind of curriculum and education they adhere to.

Speakers and influencers in the girls in STEM support movement should remember that people, often conscientious men, can feel complicit in the inequities women face and can be afraid of being blamed. The conversation of equality in STEM is never a blame game. In fact, it's a topic and discussion that enlightens participants with the power of inclusion. This EDI mindset ultimately results in innovation and personal growth, and makes everyone—including companies—richer. The approach of the conversation should always be characterized in this way.

Sometimes we don't even realize that our words, or how we say them, sound accusatory or inflict fear in others. When fear is instilled, walls will be driven up and/or defence mechanisms will be put into play. Besides introducing the topic by highlighting the importance of inclusion, you may want to alter verbiage slightly and/or to preface certain topics by announcing that there's no blame getting directed. Following a speaker session, survey a group so the respondents can remain anonymous, which results in more honest feedback. This way, you'll learn how to tweak or possibly change your presentation entirely depending on audience impression. Personally I believe it's this raw feedback—that's often hard on the ego—that makes us stronger and helps us grow professionally and personally. So don't be shy, ask for this kind of information to make sure you're delivering content that's not stimulating a culture of fear.

Over the past few years, we've seen the women in STEM movement translate into more conferences, speaker series, and initiatives rallying around supporting women, and in particular for the purpose of attracting more women into the STEM pipeline. From a motivational angle, if a presenter can inspire just one participant, then the conference is valuable. The Girls in *FIRST* Weekend is proving that such events can have an impact:

> "I believe events like the Girls in *FIRST* Weekend are so important! Events like this allow girls to network, develop friendships and support systems, and learn so much about themselves. These events allow girls to know that they have a supportive community all around them and that they can accomplish anything. The speakers allow girls to realize that it one day could be them telling their story and that nothing is impossible; they allow them to see themselves in the workplace. Most importantly, however, events like this inspire. They inspire girls to dream big and to go and make a difference within their teams and communities. They inspire girls to keep persevering and to never give up."
>
> —2018 Girls in *FIRST* Weekend participant

Many of these participants, such as those from First Nations communities, have never had a chance to experience an event such as this one. The impact can be life-changing.

> "One particular girl, who always took a leadership role in building the robot, found it very challenging last year to find her voice when speaking about her experience. This year, she has found the confidence to speak about the challenges First Nations youth face, as well as her desire to help others learn what she has learned about robotics. The Girls in *FIRST* Weekend, the space it creates for mentoring and sharing stories, has certainly played an important role in this."
>
> —Chris Mara, teacher and mentor for Wasse-Abin Wikwemikong High School First Nations robotics team

Clearly the impact of these kinds of events can be substantial, but we have to stay relevant. With the increase in such conferences, it's important to keep innovating so that content isn't simply reproduced and duplicated. Conversely, I attended an event where a participant commented, "All of these things are the same. Go, go, girls, and then you leave and you can't escape the reality that nothing is changing." It made me wonder if we're rethinking and adapting our strategy to the pace and evolution of the movement to ensure all of our hard efforts are inspiring and mobilizing the masses.

What if the content was presented in a unique way? Perhaps inviting unexpected speakers and changing up the structure would help. What if we partnered every woman panellist with a male counterpart? What if dynamic duos emerged from these partnerships where, over time, these collaborations brought us further than we've ever been before—for conference discussions, inspiration, and idea generation? In fact, I was so inspired by one such dynamic duo that I wrote a LinkedIn article about their approach. MDA Corporation's Mike Greenley and Holly Johnson presented brilliantly together about Canada's space innovation. This style of presentation can be done— and it can be done well with the right people and planning!

What if every inspirational women's conference required a quota of males in attendance? What if the same was mandated for male-dominated conferences? What if a handful of student ambassadors attended a conference circuit and listened to and observed content and presentations? What if they provided anonymous feedback on what was missing and constructive criticism for future improvement? When I polled the Girls in STEM Student Council members about STEM-panel topics, they were honest and shared with me that panels can be very boring. It was suggested that the panel include younger age groups so the audience could get a sense of the panellists' journey and could better relate to their perspective on the topic. This turned out to be a great idea that received positive feedback from both the adults and young attendees. The audience felt the panel was more relatable and inspirational, and the new method removed perceived levels of hierarchy that can sometimes exist with a panel of top-level executives.

Content-wise, how can we make panels more interactive and engaging? What about incorporating a classy game-show element that would have executives and professionals going outside their comfort zones and having a bit of fun? I'm not referring to a flashy show like Family Feud (or maybe I am?), but more like a unique, engaging framework that would go beyond just sharing the mic in often rehearsed-sounding conversation.

Conference takeaways are also a factor often not thoroughly thought through. Far too often I have left an inspiring conference without a clear next step. There may be nuggets of takeaways, but in my experience, we have never been left with a challenge, which I think could be what's needed to propel participants forward. Challenges have the potential to go viral and reach beyond the conference itself. The next conference you plan, incorporate a challenge. Get creative with it so there's a bigger chance it can be more widely shared online. For instance, ask participants to share a creative Instagram post related to a takeaway from the conference, or make a short video commentary in ode to the guest speakers. If you attend a conference that fails to include a challenge for participants to move forward with, be sure to offer that feedback to conference organizers. I've included my own list of challenges for you to take on when you finish this book!

Chapter 23: Bold Ideas to Change Culture

North American mainstream society can be inspired to change its perceptions by influencers taking action. The level of power and persuasion of certain influencers is off the charts. What if we engaged key influencers in sport, Hollywood, politics, music, business, and a vast array of other sectors to take creative action to normalize the participation of girls and women in STEM? These influencers are celebrities in their own right, and the critical component to success would be outreach to a wide variety of industries. Imagine the impact that some of these people could have on societal attitudes? Imagine if we challenged these influencers to launch creative action?

Take, for example, Will.i.am from The Black Eyed Peas, who has been a huge supporter of *FIRST* for years, helping to raise awareness of its programs. At the 2018 *FIRST* World Championship, he spoke about how amazing it would be for celebrities like J. Lo to support robotics teams. Will.i.am's involvement in robotics will raise awareness of girls in science and technology and also connect robotics with pop culture—ultimately upping the cool factor of STEM.

Dwayne "The Rock" Johnson made a video of himself teaching his two-year-old daughter Jasmine to say "girl power," and it went viral. As of the time of writing this book, the video was viewed on Instagram 27,225,802 times, and liked over 3 million times. This video took minimal effort by Johnson and, judging by the numbers, people loved it. What if we challenged Johnson to go one step further? What if his next Jasmine video was of him building a robot with her and tagging it with the hashtags #ScienceIsCool and #GirlsinSTEMRock? What if he posted a video like this once a month, showing them working on a fun STEM-related activity, and then challenged others to do it too? What if he particularly challenged dads with the hashtag #DadsforDaughtersinSTEMRock? But why on earth would he do something like this? First and foremost, I'm sure Johnson wants his daughter to have the opportunity to explore and experience all kinds of interests. Maybe his daughter is the next breakthrough AI engineer. Or maybe she will discover the cure for cancer. Or maybe she will be a Hollywood actress who will play the role of a scientist. Either way, not only would he be giving his daughter more opportunities but he'd also be showing his followers that they and their daughters can do it too, and that STEM is actually "cool." Why? Because, like him or not, Johnson is everywhere, and society has deemed him cool. Let's bring people like Johnson on board to harness that power to change our culture. Worst thing that can happen? Jasmine ends up loving LEGO robots.

Canadian producer and comedian Mike Myers still soars in popularity for his work onscreen and off. I would love to see what Mike Myers could come up with for a brilliant series on the obstacles facing girls and women in STEM—starting from a young age up to and including in the boardroom. I'm imagining smart and witty how-to clips on handling issues like microaggression that could take the heaviness of the content away and breathe some fresh, positive air into the topic, all while demonstrating how ridiculous and toxic some of these issues really are.

I'm a big fan of James Corden. Yes, he's made a living out of driving a car and singing karaoke with celebrities, but he has maintained a level of authenticity that's rare in this day and age. He's likeable and it shows in the number of fans watching his show on TV and YouTube, enjoying not just his "carpool karaoke" but his various acts of bravery, such as skydiving with Tom Cruise and performing live onstage with the Backstreet Boys. James Corden could be a huge advocate for women in STEM and he could do so with his unique flare. I would love to see him visit a woman scientist working at Gran Sasso National Laboratory and discover cool things about supernovas and dark matter. Or what about him visiting Canada's disease detective, Dr. Jennifer Gardy? James Corden is another celebrity who could bring STEM role models to the forefront.

Top CEOs and thought-leaders can lead the pack when it comes to changing the culture. We can learn a lot from watching changemakers like Microsoft CEO Satya Nadella. Satya's background of growing up in India and his many other life experiences, such as being a father to a son with brain damage, have created a leadership style based on empathy, inclusion, and innovation. I'm looking forward to seeing how Satya's diversity of thought regarding EDI, along with his approach to pushing and embracing a culture of change will resonate throughout the technology industry.

Of course there are a number of powerful woman CEOs and top executives as well who are going above and beyond to make a change. Facebook executive and LeanIn.org founder Sheryl Sandberg is dedicated to encouraging women in the STEM industry, and her books and speeches are a source of inspiration to both men and women. The more these leaders, and others in influential positions, can share their unique perspectives with others, the more they can inspire others to reach for the stars and to discover their own ways to motivate change.

Your Turn

Now it's your turn. How do we change the culture for girls in STEM? We need people of diverse backgrounds and innovative thinking to contribute. We want ideas from students, teachers, mentors, and corporate executives to share their opinion on how to make positive change.

Go to firstroboticscanada.org/voicesforchange to share your ideas.

Chapter 24: Tips for Furthering Your Career in STEM

No matter what your gender, taking steps to get noticed and further your career is critical to your growth and progress. There's a community of people who want to help you and see you succeed. You need to know when to reach out and also how to extend yourself beyond your comfort zone to get what you dream of.

From the perspective of a mentor, I know we need to provide strategies to help you move forward in your careers, despite adversities. Here are a few of my suggestions:

• When I state the importance of networking to many girls, a common response is that they're too shy and don't know how. Luckily, programs like *FIRST* Robotics Canada educate kids and youth on how to pitch an idea (and themselves) in the most effective way. I've seen the shyest of girls and boys learn to become confident and proud public speakers, anxious to take the spotlight to share their ideas. Once you have achieved that comfort, it needs to be taken one step further. You need to meet people in your chosen field and then establish a connection and get contact information. Then you must follow through and connect with that person by email or LinkedIn. I've met countless women executives who don't connect with newly made contacts on LinkedIn. I'm a big fan of LinkedIn as a form of social media, as it takes your personal status and lifestyle away from business conversations. Of course there's always that one connection who randomly posts about a delicious burger he/she just ate, but unless that burger relates to business and/or a commentary on marketing it as a product, there's no place for it on LinkedIn. Women getting into the industry have a chance for a clean slate on this platform; you can use it to communicate in a voice that expresses your knowledge and perspective about the STEM industry. Fortunately, because of services like this, you have opportunities beyond in-person networking (unlike in "the old days"), as you can do part of the work online.

• Do not underestimate the people that you know. If you do not have a high number of contacts, you can start by building on the one(s) that you already have. The one person you do know may just be the connection you need to get into a company you've been dreaming to join. Often, a close connection is overlooked because of lack of foresight into that connection's network. The only way you'll know if your contacts can truly help you in your next step is to ask them.

• Practice interviewing with real live people! In front of the mirror is also okay, but it's critical to get the public speaking experience you need so that when it's your turn to shine in the spotlight, you'll be somewhat comfortable and ready to show your stellar self. Practice interviewing for jobs but also for scholarships and grants. Practice pitching yourself as a person. Nailing the question "tell me about yourself" can be incredibly powerful. I can't count the times that I've asked this question and the response has been "what do you want to know?" Despite some disgruntled feelings about this question, I always ask it as I'm curious how candidates will respond. This is the one question you can truly get creative with; you can use it to pitch yourself in a personable and professional manner, with a little bit of leeway (as opposed to answering the more restrictive "what experience do you have?"). I particularly like hearing gems of brilliance that are unexpected and tailored to the individual. Practicing with a professional is ideal once you've worked up your confidence level, but in the meantime, your trusted friends and family are good volunteers to hear a pitch. Stand up and enjoy the moment.

• Learning to handle your emotions and stress is a must when furthering STEM education or entering the STEM job industry. Taking care of your mental state is absolutely critical to having the will and mindset to succeed. Know yourself and the people and resources that are available to you when you're in need, and never cut off the lines of communication to these contacts. Remember that you're not the only one going through tumultuous times. It may look like your peers are living the perfect life (especially when you judge by their beautiful, filter-laden pictures on social media with their hundreds of likes), but perception can be deceiving. Chances are the more frequent the beautiful posts, the more reason for them to hide the darkness they feel or are going through. We are all human and we all experience loss, hurt, anger, and times of extreme sadness. Just because we don't ultimately see this kind of emotion posted about on a regular basis doesn't mean it's not happening. So don't be too hard on yourself and assume that you're the only one going through an awkward or hard time. Have friends and family you can rely on, and also watch out for those around you who might need someone to talk to. Take care of each other.

• Never be embarrassed about a hobby or chosen career path. Too often women apologize before they even say something. I recently was talking to a high school girl in the program who, when I asked about her career path, started off by saying that "although it's really cheesy," she wanted to own her own business—a bakery. She wasn't using cheesy as a pun; she was honestly slightly embarrassed about her passion for baking. I immediately responded with words of encouragement and also reminded her that opening a bakery is a brilliant idea that will give her experience in business, finance, and marketing. Women need to stop apologizing for the things they want and to stop feeling judged for a direction that may not necessarily be accepted in society. Be a proud advocate of your aspirations—this will go a long way to helping you feel good about yourself. And the more you can express your goals, the more others can get on board and try to help you achieve them.

• Learn to take credit for your accomplishments. There's nothing wrong—and everything right—about taking credit for what you've achieved. Often women stay behind the scenes, letting moments of recognition pass them by. List your amazing professional accomplishments on sites like LinkedIn, tweet about a cool project you're working on, and most of all, be proud of what you've done—and then graciously accept compliments. Don't belittle your achievements or convince yourself they're no big deal. They are a big deal! Believe it and share it.

Chapter 25: Take the Challenge

Reading books is like attending conferences—there's always an opportunity to take a challenge. You have a chance to make a change in yourself and/or to share what you've learned with others.

Here's a list of challenges to choose from (a gold star for those keeners who tackle them all!):

• For your next baby shower, give a gift that doesn't conform to gender stereotyping. Not attending a baby shower in the near future? Share this challenge with someone who is!

• Similar to the first challenge, choose a toy for a boy or girl that he or she might not receive from someone else because it's not stereotypical. It's okay for boys to receive fluffy stuffed animals just as it is for girls to play with building blocks and trucks.

• If you happen to be strolling in a kids' clothing section and you see a shirt that says anything like "I'm a girl. I don't do math," then ask to speak to the store manager immediately. Ask them why they're promoting such a product.

• Encourage a girl to join a robotics club! If she doesn't know how to build a robot or thinks she can't do it, pick up a small robot kit and build it with her to prove she can.

• When you're asked what movie you want to see, be equipped with the list of recommended movies in this book—especially if you're watching with a young girl.

• Talk to boys about how working with women as equal partners will be mutually beneficial and the best way to get things done—as well as absolutely normal.

• Read a book to a loved one. Whether the listener is young or old, books can offer hope, change perceptions, and open minds to new possibilities

• Ask a young person what he or she thinks about science. Whether he/she thinks it's fun or not so fun, ask him/her the reason for the answer.

• Take a moment and look up the Classy Cyborgs and their extraordinary innovation to help solve the Braille literacy crisis. Read, reflect, and consider the potential of talented preteens who are given opportunities in STEM.

• Think about how a leader at your work, school, or robotics club influences others. Is this leader renowned for uplifting those around him or her? As part of this team, how can you contribute to making positive change?

• Pay attention to the language that you use. Stop yourself from using "guys" when referencing a group of people. Replace "guys" with "everyone" or a gender-neutral term.

• Brainstorm a list of jobs that are traditionally categorized for men or women (for example, nurses are still often thought of as women). Is this perception changing? Engage in a fruitful debate with someone who cares and come up with brilliant ideas on how you can help change this.

• Always remember that kids have an amazing sense of hearing. Just when you think it's impossible for them to overhear your private conversation, you'll find it's not. Be cognizant of your attitudes and the words you use. One off-the-cuff comment could affect someone for life.

• When you witness microaggression at school, work, or home, politely draw attention to it. Too often we sit back and take a passive attitude towards this kind of behaviour, yet microsponsorship could be the key to transforming negative situations into learning experiences and to changing team culture.

• If you are a part of a team, club, workplace, or any type of organization, check to see if a code of conduct exists. If it doesn't, work as a group to create one as a team-building exercise. Then be sure it's accessible and available on your website.

• Look outside yourself and your own needs and take interest in others. Ask how someone is doing and focus your full attention on his or her answer. Giving someone your time and a listening ear can go a long way to building relationships and making someone's day.

• Whether you're a student or a facilitator, keep in mind the importance of questions. There's usually at least one person in a group who has a question but is not asking due to low self-confidence or embarrassment. As a facilitator, pay attention and draw questions or comments out of your participants.

• No matter your age, you have the opportunity to be a role model to someone else. Whether you're in high school or a part of the workforce, remember there's always someone who needs help and support.

• Highlight the arts when it comes to promoting STEM. Don't let a creative and artistically inclined individual write off a career in STEM due to lack of knowledge about related opportunities.

• We all know someone who's a perfectionist. When you witness perfectionist tendencies severely impacting an individual, try and remind him or her that exploration is better than perfection.

• The busier we get, the easier it is to be remiss about finding support for ourselves mentally. Take care of yourself. And also be aware of others around you who may appreciate the support network you're a part of.

• Celebrate a champion of change! Send a thank-you note or write a blog post and share the good news story with others.

• The next time you sit down before a meeting, look around and identify who is not participating in conversation. Try and pull them into discussion and engage everyone.

• If your club or organization is recruiting new members, don't underestimate the power of words and writing style. Remember that nice-to-have qualifications should be written as just that, instead of seeming like must-haves. This way, you may receive applicants from a more diverse talent pool.

• Patience is one of the best characteristics of a mentor. Pack your patience when in teaching mode and remember that it only takes one moment to spark creativity and ingenuity in a student. Make your moments count.

• Remember to keep an open mind and attitude when discussing topics like gender equality. The point is not to blame but rather to collaborate and find innovative strategies and solutions.

• You don't have to be officially employed as a marketer to understand and apply EDI learning to promotional campaigns. Whether you're spreading word about a product, organization, or team, EDI is relevant to all marketing initiatives.

• Recommend that your team do EDI training. Choose a training program that you feel is appropriate for the group and challenge each team member to enroll, and then schedule an open discussion as a follow-up.

• Councils and committees should have representation and voices from diverse communities, reflecting a multitude of experiences. Be careful that your council does not have too many members with similar voices, as you can risk missing out on diverse perspectives, which are needed to strengthen the chance of innovation and the change you can make as a group.

• Approach conference planning with an EDI lens—not just from a gender equality point of view, but from the perspective of traditionally underrepresented groups.

Remember, the only way we have a chance at changing our culture is if we use our collective intelligence and forward-thinking attitudes to share our voices and ideas in order to implement a shift in perceptions. We must provide the resources and environment for the next generation to implement effective and innovative strategies to make changes that will benefit everyone. We have all witnessed the power and drive of today's brilliant students. Even when we experience some of our darkest doubts that this type of change is impossible, remember these exceptional kids. We have the power to inspire them to be the kinds of leaders and changemakers who will change our culture. Start by demonstrating to them the kind of attitudes and behaviours that truly can make a difference.

For more resources and information about *FIRST* Robotics Canada and girls in STEM, visit firstroboticscanada.org.

Proceeds of this book will be donated to *FIRST* Robotics Canada's equity, diversity, and inclusion initiatives.

Connect with author Kim Cooper on LinkedIn, Twitter, and Instagram @kimucooper.

Acknowledgements

First and foremost, thank you to those who shared their stories that motivated me to compile ideas for change. I'm thankful for the opportunity to work closely with talented students who inspire me to make a difference every day—no matter how big or small.

Thank you to Dr. Imogen Coe, Dorothy Byers, Mark Breadner, Sarah Howden and Jill Monsod who exercised the utmost patience as I worked through the process of reflection and revisions.

I'm eternally grateful to have a tight-knit group of believers who fuel my energy and push me to new heights, despite numerous wipeouts along the way. My parents Steve and Jo-Anne Cooper always believe in me and guide me to look past the naysayers, focus on my passion, and maintain my resolution to make positive changes in this world. Tracy Cooper, Ryan Banfield, and Charles Banfield have taught me to be bold, original, and true to myself.

A very special thanks to my best friend Corina Lloyd who endures my grandiose raves and rants, and is there for me no matter what life brings. A shout-out to my handsome rescue dog Micki who managed to stay awake and alert while I read aloud multiple revisions of my book.

Finally, I want to recognize forces of inspiration who energize me on a daily basis: John Abele, Lesley Breeze, Raman Dang, Arti Javeri, Dr. Douglas Jay, Paul Keenan, Sheri Lynn Koscielski, Heather McDermott, Kevin Murai, Annika Pint, Laura Rietveld, Sylvan Scott, Mike Sinnaeve, Moru Wang, the entire staff at *FIRST* Robotics Canada, and to the best Nan ever who'll always be missed, Nellie Convey.

About the Author

Kim Cooper is the vice president of partnerships at *FIRST* Robotics Canada, a charity encouraging kids and youth in science, technology, engineering, and math (STEM). Kim is also co-chair of the Girls in STEM Executive Advisory Council and was recognized as an inspiring Canadian leader in business and technology. She's passionate about sharing the stories of underrepresented youth and is part of the movement to bring equity, diversity, and inclusivity (EDI) into the STEM fields. Kim is a freelance writer for Scholastic Education, as well as a business instructor at Sheridan College. Kim's career experience ranges from editor of a kids' magazine to digital producer for youth media. Her educational background is in business, writing, and Japanese.